Dear Mom

A Keepsake *of* Blessings *and* Memories
of Growing Up with You

Ellie Claire®
gift & paper expressions

...inspired by life
EllieClaire.com

Ellie Claire® Gift & Paper Expressions
Brentwood, TN 37027
EllieClaire.com
Ellie Claire is a registered trademark of Worthy Media, Inc.

Dear Mom Journal
© 2014 by Ellie Claire
Published by Ellie Claire, an imprint of Worthy Publishing Group, a division of Worthy Media, Inc.

ISBN 978-1-60936-921-7

Scripture is taken from: The Holy Bible, New International Version®, NIV® Copyright © 1973, 1978, 1984, 2011 by Biblica, Inc.® All rights reserved worldwide. The Holy Bible, New King James Version® (NKJV). Copyright © 1982 by Thomas Nelson, Inc. The Holy Bible, New Living Translation (NLT) copyright © 1996, 2004, 2007 by Tyndale House Foundation. Used by permission of Tyndale House Publishers Inc., Carol Stream, Illinois 60188. *The Message* (MSG). Copyright © 1993, 1994, 1995, 1996, 2000, 2001, 2002. Used by permission of NavPress Publishing Group. Used by permission. All rights reserved.

Stock or custom editions of Ellie Claire titles may be purchased in bulk for educational, business, ministry, fundraising, or sales promotional use. For information, please e-mail info@EllieClaire.com

Cover and interior design by Jeff and Lisa Franke | www.art-lab-studios.com

Printed in China

1 2 3 4 5 6 7 8 9 – 19 18 17 16 15 14

*D*ear Mom, I thank God
for the blessing you are...
for the joy of your laughter...
the comfort of your prayers...
the warmth of your smile.

Dear Mom,

This journal is just for us. It captures all my memories
and blessings of growing up with you. Some are funny,
some are sweet, some are bittersweet, some are surprising,
but all are reflections of my love for you.

There will be pages with full comments and some with short
comments and some with no comments. But whether long
or short, all the bits and pieces have been personalized
specifically to create a one-of-a-kind keepsake just for you.

This gift comes from my heart. Thank you for all you have done,
are doing, and will do for me. I am blessed to call you Mother.

Remember When...

There are cherished memories that I have tucked away to pull out and relive when I'm away or lonely or just need a "mom" moment—the "remember when?" times that brought us to tears either with laughter or sadness. The family get-togethers that we can never forget. The just-you-and-me moments that have made our relationship extra special. These are the shared memories I will always remember.

I thank my God every time I remember you.
In all my prayers for...you, I always pray with joy.

PHILIPPIANS 1:3 NIV

Remember when I wanted to be a...

*R*emember when you taught me to...

*R*emember when we laughed so hard about...

....

....

....

....

....

....

....

....

....

....

....

....

....

....

$\mathcal{R}$emember when I would watch you while you...

$\mathcal{R}$emember the family get-together when...

*R*emember when I got so mad because..

Remember when I tried to fix the broken...

*R*emember when we surprised...

*R*emember when we went on vacation and...

*R*emember when you told me about God...

*R*emember when we talked all the time about...

$\mathcal{R}$emember that movie I watched (or book I read) over and over.....................

*R*emember when I had a sleepover and...

....

....

....

....

....

....

....

....

....

....

....

....

....

....

....

....

....

*R*emember when I first realized God could use me to...

....

....

....

....

....

....

....

....

....

....

....

....

....

....

....

....

....

....

NOTES, PHOTOS, CARDS

My Favorite Things

As my mom, you know many of my favorite things. But there are some that may surprise you. This list includes a lot of my favorites, from the food that we ate to the birthday that is imprinted in my memory forever. Everything on this list pales in comparison to my very favorite thing on Earth—you!

We thank you, God, we thank you—your Name is our favorite word; your mighty works are all we talk about.

PSALM 75:1 MSG

My favorite memory of you is...

$\mathcal{M}$y favorite meal you ever made was..

My favorite thing to wear all the time was..

....

....

....

....

....

....

....

....

....

....

....

....

....

....

$\mathscr{M}$y favorite holiday tradition is...

$\mathscr{M}$y favorite gift you ever gave me is...

$\mathcal{M}$y favorite family vacation was...

My favorite room in our house growing up has to be..

....

....

....

....

....

....

....

....

....

....

....

....

....

....

....

....

$\mathcal{M}$y favorite expression you use a lot is...

*M*y favorite candy that I always begged for was...

$\mathcal{M}$y favorite birthday memory is...

*M*y favorite family pet is/was..

....

....

....

....

....

....

....

....

....

....

....

....

....

....

....

....

$\mathcal{M}$y favorite place to hide was...

*M*y favorite song you sang is..

....

....

....

....

....

....

....

....

....

....

....

....

....

....

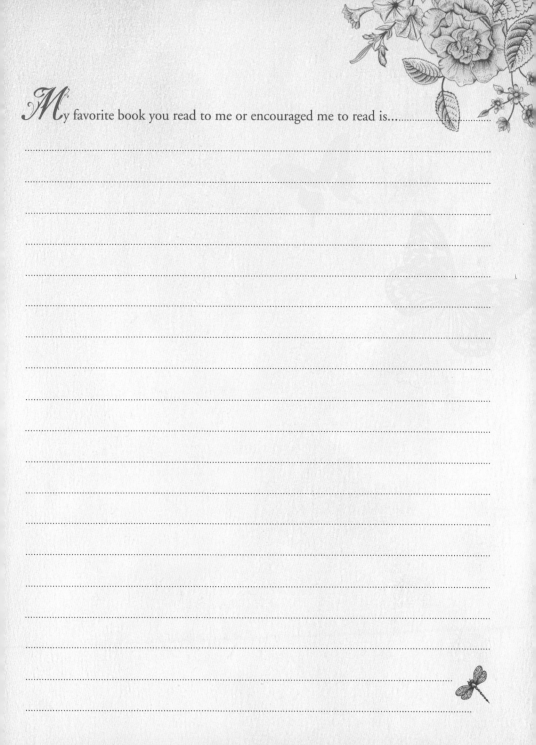

$\mathcal{M}$y favorite book you read to me or encouraged me to read is...

We Are Stronger Because...

In every life there are things that are hard to get through.
Thankfully for me, I had you as a mom to help guide me through
the tough patches. You taught me lessons that made the hard
things bearable, and showed me, through love and by example,
that hard things can be used by God to make us stronger.
For that, I am extremely grateful.

*We know that in all things God works for the good of those
who love him, who have been called according to his purpose.*

Romans 8:28 niv

The hardest thing I ever had to tell you was...

*O*ur family had to navigate a tough time when...

The time I saw you sacrifice for our family was...

The time I saw you give sacrificially for others was…………………………………………………………………

The difficult time in our family when you demonstrated grace was.............................

....

....

....

....

....

....

....

....

....

....

....

....

....

....

....

The thing that most frightened me and how you made it better was.....................

I regret the time I made you feel...

You helped me over that embarrassing moment...

The punishment I remember most is..

....

....

....

....

....

....

....

....

....

....

....

....

....

....

....

....

The challenge I remember you struggling through for God was...

You helped me overcome problems in school by..

The thing about myself I don't like but you are helping me accept is...

....

....

....

....

....

....

....

....

....

....

....

....

....

....

....

....

....

....

....

....

The hardest thing about leaving home was..

The purpose I am seeing in my life because of you is..

NOTES, PHOTOS, CARDS

Lessons Learned

Even though I may not have expressed it often, I am thankful for all the lessons you've taught me. We haven't always agreed but I knew that you loved me and wanted the best for me. So you taught me lessons. Some I got right away. Some I am still learning. Thank you for continuing to teach me.

I applied my heart to what I observed
and learned a lesson from what I saw.

PROVERBS 24:32 NIV

The best lesson you ever taught me was...

*T*he lesson about faith I most appreciate is...

The adage you repeated to me over and over that I wish I had listened to is...............

....

....

....

....

....

....

....

....

....

....

....

....

....

....

....

....

The lesson that was hardest for me to learn is...

You taught me to respect others by..

....

....

....

....

....

....

....

....

....

....

....

....

....

....

....

The most important lesson you taught me about money was...

The nugget of wisdom I have cherished to this day is..

....

....

....

....

....

....

....

....

....

....

....

....

....

....

....

....

The lesson about the importance of family was demonstrated when...

....

....

....

....

....

....

....

....

....

....

....

....

....

....

....

....

....

....

....

You taught me compassion by..

....

....

....

....

....

....

....

....

....

....

....

....

....

....

....

....

*Y*ou taught me to accept my flaws by...

You taught me the importance of thinking before I act when...

....

....

....

....

....

....

....

....

....

....

....

....

....

....

The lesson I learned a little too publicly was...

The lesson I'm still trying to learn is..

The best advice you ever gave me was...

NOTES, PHOTOS, CARDS

Stories I Love

There are stories you have told that touch my heart;
stories that make me smile or roar with laughter.
Stories about grandparents and family and other people
who have come in and out of our lives. And there
are stories that I tell my friends about this wonderful
family we are part of. Here are a few of my favorites.

I will teach you hidden lessons from our past—
stories we have heard and known,
stories our ancestors handed down to us.

PSALM 78:2–3 NLT

*M*y favorite story to tell is..

....

....

....

....

....

....

....

....

....

....

....

....

....

....

....

....

The story I love about your kindness is...

The story I tell others when they ask about my mom is...................................

....

....

....

....

....

....

....

....

....

....

....

....

....

....

....

$\mathcal{M}$y favorite story that you told me is..

The story of an adventure that scared me silly but now makes me laugh is..................

....

....

....

....

....

....

....

....

....

....

....

....

....

....

....

....

The wild and crazy side of you is best seen in the story about...

....

....

....

....

....

....

....

....

....

....

....

....

....

....

....

....

....

....

....

....

*M*y favorite story of you growing up is...

*M*y favorite story you tell about me when I was little is...

....

....

....

....

....

....

....

....

....

....

....

....

....

....

....

....

The story about the best day of growing up with you for a mom is.............................

....

....

....

....

....

....

....

....

....

....

....

....

....

....

....

....

The accident story that I'll never forget is...

The story about our family get-together that still makes me chuckle is............................

....

....

....

....

....

....

....

....

....

....

....

....

....

....

....

....

*M*y favorite car story is...

*T*he holiday story that I remember most is...

....

....

....

....

....

....

....

....

....

....

....

....

....

....

....

....

....

*M*y favorite story told by a family member is..

NOTES, PHOTOS, CARDS

Relatives and Family Friends

Friends and family come in all shapes and sizes,
moods and dispositions, characters and personalities.
We've shared some great times, some hard times,
and some really memorable times with this cast of characters.
Thank you for allowing them to shape my life.

*Her neighbors and relatives heard that the Lord
had shown her great mercy, and they shared her joy.*

Luke 1:58 niv

The relative that makes me laugh the hardest is..

....

....

....

....

....

....

....

....

....

....

....

....

....

....

The most memorable family in our neighborhood was...

....

....

....

....

....

....

....

....

....

....

....

....

....

....

....

....

....

The friends that have always loved me like I'm family are...

The family road trip I remember most is...

The holiday that is best shared with the whole family is...

....

....

....

....

....

....

....

....

....

....

....

....

....

....

....

....

....

The food we always have to eat at family get-togethers is

*T*he things I like best about your side of the family is..

....

....

....

....

....

....

....

....

....

....

....

....

....

....

....

....

....

The traits I inherited from our family that I love are...

....

....

....

....

....

....

....

....

....

....

....

....

....

....

....

....

....

$\mathcal{O}$ur family is well-known for...

That thing about our family that makes me most proud is...

The friends that we shared life with while I was growing up were...

....

....

....

....

....

....

....

....

....

....

....

....

....

....

....

....

....

....

....

The funniest friend we had as a family was...

The family member who we most often tried to avoid was..

....

....

....

....

....

....

....

....

....

....

....

....

....

....

....

....

....

The friends or family members we most anticipated visiting were...

....

....

....

....

....

....

....

....

....

....

....

....

....

....

....

....

....

....

....

....

....

....

....

NOTES, PHOTOS, CARDS

I Am So Thankful for You

More than anything, I am grateful to have you as my mom.
We might not have been the perfect family, but we were perfect
for each other. Thank you for just being Mom, for loving me
unconditionally, for seeing in me things I could not see myself,
for protecting me as I grew up in ways I cannot even now
understand. From the bottom of my heart, I want to thank you
for all you've done and all you've meant to me.

I give you thanks, O Lord, with all my heart.

PSALM 138:1 NLT

I am most grateful for your...

I am grateful and really proud of the way you helped our family by...

I am grateful for your ability to make me smile when you...

....

....

....

....

....

....

....

....

....

....

....

....

....

....

....

I am grateful for the relationships you modeled, like...

_____

_____

_____

_____

_____

_____

_____

_____

_____

_____

_____

_____

_____

_____

_____

I am grateful for the prayers you've prayed for me and with me, especially...........

I am grateful for when you indulged me by...

....

....

....

....

....

....

....

....

....

....

....

....

....

....

....

....

....

....

I am grateful for the time you cheered me on by...

....

....

....

....

....

....

....

....

....

....

....

....

....

....

_I_ am grateful for how you make me feel beautiful by...

I am grateful for when you stood up for what you knew was right by.........................

....

....

....

....

....

....

....

....

....

....

....

....

....

....

....

I am grateful for how you influenced my personal faith by...

....

....

....

....

....

....

....

....

....

....

....

....

....

....

....

....

I am grateful for being alive after I...
....
....
....
....
....
....
....
....
....
....
....
....
....
....

I am grateful for the bandages and kisses when…

I am grateful that you let me try...

....

....

....

....

....

....

....

....

....

....

....

....

....

....

....

I am grateful that you were there for me when..

NOTES, PHOTOS, CARDS

In My Own Words

There are some things that I just have to tell you—
things that are unique to our relationship. Or photos
that I want to show you with explanations or captions,
memories of my life with you. Or doodles I couldn't help
but draw of fun times or family trees that I think you'll enjoy.
In the next few pages, I want to let you know how much I love
and appreciate you...in my own words and in my own way.

These things we write to you that your joy may be full.

1 JOHN 1:4 NKJV